101 TIPS TO BE A FANTASTIC TRAVEL NANNY

101 pieces of advice and information for nannies, travel nannies and would-be nannies, who will be travelling or going on holiday with children.

Contents

Chapter 1. Introduction

Having nannied and taught children for over ten years, I rather fell into the role of a travel nanny. As a newly qualified teacher, I was looking for inspiration on travelling cheaply in the run up to my first summer holiday. During my research I came across the concept of a travel nanny. Since then I have accompanied numerous families on their holidays. These have included beach holidays to the South of France, city breaks in London, skiing in Switzerland and even a wedding in Barbados! The children have ranged in age from 6months to 14 years old and I have thoroughly enjoyed every experience so far.

Initially, it was a challenge to gather advice and expectations regarding the role of a travel nanny. Ten years ago, it was a rather novel concept to have a travel nanny. Much of the advice within these pages was learnt through first-hand experience. Additionally, I have received some great advice over the years from My Travelling Nanny (mytravellingnanny.co.uk), an agency who specialises in providing holiday and travelling nannies to families.

Nowadays, there is a much greater demand among families for a travel nanny to accompany them on their holidays. Thus, I wrote this guide in the hope it would be of use to current or prospective travel nannies by providing advice and ideas. The advice and ideas range from securing the perfect holiday nanny job to specific advice for holidays at the beach or ski resorts. Parents who are considering hiring a travel nanny or will be travelling themselves with children for the first time will also find the following pages beneficial I hope.

I would like to thank my family and friends for all their continued support during my career so far. And thank you to all the amazing children I've encountered and had the privilege of teaching and looking after.

I hope you find the following pages useful and informative.

Chapter 2. Applying for Travel Nanny Jobs

1. Decide on the sort of travel nanny job you want. Is it short term to work around other career commitments or long term where you could be away for a few months or a year at a time.

2. Make sure your CV is up-to-date and demonstrates your experience and skills that are especially useful for a travel nanny. Experience of working abroad in any capacity should be mentioned. Any level of proficiency in a language should be highlighted. Sporting skills such as the ability to ski and being a competent and confident swimmer are especially beneficial.

3. If lacking current experience relevant to the role of a travel nanny, try and gain some. Offer your services to family or friends at a (possibly very) discounted rate. Even a short overnight break, regardless of the distance all counts as experience gained. Experience such as accompanying school children on a school trip or working on a residential summer camp is valuable too. Ask for advice from other travel nannies about how they built up experience. Facebook Groups such as Jet Set Nannies are great for asking for advice, picking up tips and becoming au fait with the different variety of travel nanny jobs that are available.

4. Don't give up if you are initially rejected for jobs. Ask for some feedback and keep trying! Apart from applying to agencies through their websites think about using a site such as LinkedIn to job search as well. Initially, it is best to sign up to an agency as they are the experts who can keep you informed of possible employment, offer advice and ensure all goes as smoothly as possible. Agencies will also try to match you with the families they see as 'a best fit' in terms of experience and personality. Another possibility is creating an advert on sites such as Gumtree (Gumtree charge a small monthly fee). Be creative – word of mouth, adverts in newspapers – anyway you can think of that will get help you get your start in the travel nanny industry.

Chapter 3. Organisation Before Departure

You have booked the job – well done! Now you need to organise yourself, prepare for your travels and the upcoming job. Fail to prepare, prepare to fail!

5. Always have a contract (however informal it may be!) which sets out exactly the arrangements made between you and your employing family. This ensures a degree of formality and keeps you right as to expectations for pay, hours etc. A contract also ensures a degree of accountability if anything should go wrong. Template contracts are available online.

6. Investigate travel insurance. Some employers pay it, some expect you to have your own travel insurance. If you end up working as a travel nanny regularly it is worth investing in an annual travel insurance. This is also an impressive extra to highlight to potential employers.

7. Ensure that Enhanced Disclosure Checks (CRB/DBS) are updated at least every 3 years and that your First Aid training is up to date. If you don't have a First Aid certification it is advisable to get one. There are some agencies who will not put you forward for possible jobs until you have completed First Aid Training.

8. Ask questions about the family and children beforehand – for example eating habits, likes and dislikes, allergies, routines. This is so important if travel nannying with a family for the first time. Make sure that you are well-prepared and well-informed, so you can anticipate any problems and get to know the family and their habits as quickly as possible. Also, if a family adheres to a certain religion or certain eating habits e.g. veganism it is always useful to know this in advance.

9. Following on from the above - communication is key. Prepare a list of questions ready to ask the employing family when appropriate. How involved and hands on do the parents want you to be? Will it be sole care, shared care or a mixture of both? Would they like activities planned and a daily routine mapped

out? Will you have a room to yourself or share with the children?
As a rule, if you are sharing with children then an additional
supplement should be added for this.   What is their approach
when it comes to discipline? Are they currently toilet training?
Are they celebrating any special occasions e.g. a birthday?

10. Do some research on the destination in hand – weather, culture,
    language etc. If you're staying in a hotel it is a good to research
    the facilities e.g. a hairdryer, free WIFI etc. so you know what to
    bring and what facilities are available

11. If the country's language is different to your own its worth
    investing in a language app – Babel and VidaLingua are worth
    checking out.

12. Check your passport is up-to-date. There are some countries
    outside Europe that require your passport to have 6 months
    validity.

13. Check if the country you are entering requires a visa - your
    employer should be reimbursing you for the cost of the visa or
    applying for it on your behalf.

14. Following on from the above check if you require any
    vaccinations or if there is any travel advice concerning the place
    you are travelling to. If vaccinations are required again this is
    something your employer should be paying or reimbursing you for.

15. Check insurance policies for your mobile phone or other
    valuables – around children and by the beach or pool accidents are
    liable to happen!

16. Pack appropriately – weather, activities, adaptors etc. It is also
    worth asking your employers if there is any specific clothing you

need to bring e.g. smart dresses, trainers, swimsuits, ski gear. Check luggage allowances!

17. When it comes to your own luggage my motto is now cheap and cheerful. Having learnt the hard way when designer sunglasses have been sat on and watches have been scratched I now have my economy travel versions of sunglasses, watches, clothes and jewellery.

18. Pack snacks. It is always wise if travelling with a family on a long journey to bring food with you just in case of delays or not liking airport or plane food. A hungry nanny is a less effective (and maybe cranky) nanny!

19. Plan your journey to the family/airport appropriately. If meeting at the airport, make sure you are there on time if not early. As a rule, I try and arrive at least 20 minutes ahead of schedule then relax with a coffee and am not stressed or worried about arriving late.

20. If relevant take a small amount of the local currency,

21. Leave your contact details, emergency contact details, travel details and itinerary with at least one other person - in case of emergencies!

22. Make sure your employers also have an emergency contact for you in case of accidents and emergencies.

Chapter 4. Enroute

Some holidays you will meet the family at the chosen holiday destination, others you will travel with the family. On occasions, there might even be times when you are travelling solo with the children from one parent to another. If travelling with a family expect to be working. Your job is to make their holiday more fun, relaxed and an even more enjoyable experience for them as a family. When travelling on a long plane/train/car with the family these tips should help:

23. At some point when travelling choose an appropriate moment to discuss how to assemble any equipment such as prams, Manducas, travel cots etc.

24. If travelling with a baby or young child make sure they are fed, watered and their nappy changed before the journey starts. It could be a while before you get the chance to change them again.

25. On planes ask the flight attendant the whereabouts of the changing table as aircraft tend to only have one toilet with a designated baby changing area.

26. On occasions a travel nanny will be accompanying a parent who perhaps does not do the majority of parenting and might not be used to the long list of 'stuff' babies and small children need. It is a great idea to bring your own small bag of essentials and extras e.g. tissues, hand sanitizer, wipes, soothers, distractors.

27. Bring some age appropriate forms of entertainment with you if you can. Employers appreciate this as it shows your pro-activeness and thoughtfulness. It doesn't have to be many things or anything particularly fancy or expensive, but every bit helps! Packs of cards, books, soft toys, paper and crayons – the excitement of something 'NEW' with which to be entertained always helps.

28. Make sure young children are comfy and settled for travelling. Small details such as taking off shoes, swapping jeans for tracksuit bottoms, loosening belts and using blankets and pillows all contribute to the settling process.

29. Try and build up a positive relationship with the children from the start. It can be difficult when you have just met but using encouraging positive phrases and praising them for behaving well always help. Asking questions regarding their likes and dislikes, favourite foods, favourite colour etc. all helps establish a positive relationship.

30. If travelling with a baby a Manduca is always useful to soothe and settle.

31. Throughout the journey remain proactive. Asking your employers if there is anything else you can do throughout the journey to help is always appreciated. Communication throughout the holiday is key!

32. Stay on top of the little tasks while travelling e.g. rinsing out used bottles, bagging up used clothes, wiping down toys with sanitizing wipes.

33. Bring a clean top or maybe a change of clothes for yourself - the chances of you reaching your destination without spillage or stains is slim. Trust me!!

34. If travelling together with a family, make sure you ask for their approach to discipline. Some families like to be the only authority figure when everyone is together, some are happy for you to do it in tandem with them.

35. If travelling solo with children record any important details in a notebook or make notes on your phone. Include what they ate, nap times, nappy changes etc.

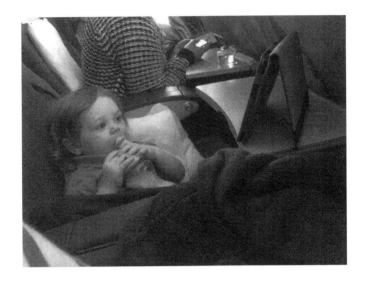

Chapter 5. Accommodation

Advice for when you reach your accommodation:

36. If jet lag is a possibility try and stay up a bit later and do
     something active. If you are in a different time zone be prepared
     that meal times might different to normal. Having healthy snacks
     to hand for the children will help combat this if meal times are
     slightly out of sync.

37. Get to know your surroundings quickly by carrying out a quick
     risk assessment.   In a hotel check for the emergency exits. If

staying in a villa check if there is a main road close by. Always have a scan for anything that might pose a danger.

38. If looking after a baby or very young child try and 'baby proof' the accommodation as far as possible. An effective and cheap method is using duct tape to cover electrical outlets or soften sharp edges.

39. Personal boundaries. Depending on your personality and the children it is a good idea to set certain personal boundaries. For example, if you are in a villa with your own room are you happy for the children to come into your bedroom. If not, you need to tell them that from the start. Or if sharing a room with the children make sure they know that they have to ask permission before touching your belongings.

40. If you will be helping prepare the meals for children get into the kitchen and see what kitchen equipment is available – not all accommodation types will have everything you expect/want.

41. Prepare to be flexible. The family are on holiday, so the same routines and schedules can't be expected – flexibility is key. However, asking the night before about plans for the day, responsibilities, requests etc. ensures that everyone is on the same page and has a general idea of how the day will go.

42. Discuss petty cash/expenses. Do they want you to keep receipts if you are buying treats for the children etc. or will they give you petty cash for the duration of the holiday?

43. On self-catering holidays, the family will most likely want help with meal preparation. Hopefully, you will have already been given a list of potential meals that the children will enjoy and eat – but if not then ask. Try and stick to healthy straightforward meals that can be prepared easily and quickly. A quick internet surf will help with any searches for suggestions!

44. My go-to-activity for engaging with children 3years and upwards is some sort of treasure hunt or scavenger hunt – a sure fire hit with any age of children.

45. One of the biggest perks of having a travel nanny is having an evening babysitter so parents can go out at night, safe in the knowledge their children are being well-looked after. Ensuring you have a knowledge of their bedroom routine, where the parents are going and how they can be contacted are necessities. Send a message when the children are settled, showered and asleep etc. will ease apprehension for parents.

46. A night-time routine is particularly important for children who are not familiar with you. Try also to integrate some sort of positive behavior reward within this. A holiday nighttime routine will help settle children into sleeping well in a strange place.

47. Continuing from the above a tablet device can be very useful for settling children in unfamiliar circumstances in several ways. Reading a bedtime story, playing some music, perhaps even 10/15 minutes of a programme to send them over to asleep. Make sure you check with employers before using a tablet device you have brought if they do not have their own.

48. Always end the day on a positive note when children go to bed – continuously building a positive relationship is so important. A stock phrase I use with children of any age on travel nanny trips is 'Thanks for a great day – I really enjoyed the fun we had and thank you for being so well-behaved and having brilliant manners.' If they do happen to have repeated behavioral issues modify the sentence as appropriate but keep it positive such as 'Thank you for a fun day and doing your best to behave well.'

49. Have your own entertainment prepared if you are babysitting most evenings. Especially with a young child there might be lots of time when they are sleeping, and you are house-bound.

50. Ending the day with your employer by asking 'Is there anything else I can do before I go...' is a very positive way of both politely letting your employer know that your time is up but also that you are willing to do any last tasks before you finish your work for the day.

Chapter 6. Sun Holiday V Ski Holiday

Holidays mean different types of things to certain people. However, most of the holidays a travel nanny accompanies a family on involve either the sun and relaxation, or the snow and skiing. Here are some relevant tips depending the destination

Sun Holiday

51. On a sun holiday, children must be sun-creamed regularly. Set reminders on your watch or phone for when sun cream will need to be topped up.

52. Bring talcum powder to the beach. Applying talcum powder helps to brush the sand off easily be reapplying sun cream.

53. At the beach or pool bring frozen water bottles that will melt during the day or use vacuum bottles. Cold water to keep children hydrated throughout the day is essential.

54. If you have sole charge of the children for a day make sure the children are not over-exposed to the sun during the hottest part of the day (11am-3pm). If they are out then they should be covered up with clothes, sunhat and sunglasses.

55. At the beach locate the lifeguard and ask them where the safest place is for children to swim, paddle or dip their toes in the water. They are the experts and will be able to advise you.

56. Pack a bag with essentials before heading to the pool or beach. This should include sun cream, sunglasses, snacks, drinks, games, change of clothes, extra swim suits in case of accidents, chill out activities in the shade. Additionally, bring a waterproof wet bag

where you can store wet swim-clothes at the end of the day without everything else getting wet too.

57. At the beach or pool the safety of the children is the priority. If they are near the water you should be too, if they are in the water you should be in the water too. It is scary how quickly a small child could potentially fall into the pool or be knocked off their feet by a wave. When water is involved, vigilance at all times is key.

58. At the beach or pool '10minute chill out sessions' are a good idea for children. Keep them in the shade and hydrate them. Make sure you have entertainment to hand also.

59. If you have a baby or small child at the beach having a small inflatable pool is a great way of bringing the water to them without the waves or other dangers of the sea. A few inches of water in their pool and a some toys can lead to hours of contentment and fun.

60. At the end of a pool/beach session use the showers to rinse off pool water or sea water and have a change of clothes available. Overexposure to chlorine and sand can cause irritation to the skin.

61. Be prepared in advance with a list of fun activities – sand castle competitions, scavenger lists, treasure hints in the pool, hand-stand competitions etc.

62. Clean out the beach bag at the end of every day. Rinse the swimming costumes, dust off the sand, empty the wet bag and replenish the snacks. Check there is adequate sun cream for the whole of the next day. This is the sort of attention to detail that employers will appreciate.

63. Bring simple, healthy and easy to eat snacks for the children to the beach or pool e.g. fruit, vegetable sticks, boxes of raisins,

energy bars, pretzels. There are lots of great beach snack ideas on Pinterest.

Ski Holidays:

64. Layers, layers, layers. Ensure children have enough layers on when out and about and skiing on the slopes. Bring extra layers in a small rucksack so more layers can be added, or layers can be taken off if at some stage they get too warm.

65. If possible, try to name all items of clothing - gloves and hats especially are likely to go astray. Named clothing will increase the chances of the clothing making its way back you and the family at some stage! I keep a Sharpie in my handbag for a quick ad hoc naming of clothes (obviously ask permission first!).

66. Stay organised – have a named box/basket for each child where they can stash their ski mitts, hats, buffs etc. after skiing. This will reduce time and effort before the next ski session and helps in promoting ownership and responsibility for possessions among children.

67. Lie out all the ski clothing needed the night before. This will save time in the morning.

68. If heading outside always check the weather forecast first. Weather apps are great to have on your phone. The weather can change very quickly up a mountain and you don't want to be caught up in heavy snowfall or a blizzard.

69. Check if there is a First Aid kit within your accommodation and that it is packed with plasters, anti-septic cream, blister gel, muscle gel and so on. If your ski chalet does not have a First Aid Kit you should ask for one or offer to go and purchase a few items to make an ad hoc First Aid kit.

70. Remember to pack a mini sun cream when skiing and apply to exposed areas including on lips. It is easy to pick up sunburn

without even realising it on the slopes. Having a lip balm with inbuilt sun protection is also very useful as lips can chap easily in the cold weather.

71. If out skiing with children make sure you have snacks, a small First Aid kit and spare layers of clothing in your rucksack.

72. Before going skiing with children have a brief safety chat. Outline a few points e.g. how far ahead can they ski in front of you and have an emergency meeting point incase anyone gets separated.

73. It is always helpful to have an emergency contact card details attached to every child. This should include their name, medical conditions, your contact details, family contact details, emergency meeting point, where they are staying and emergency contact details.

74. During ski sessions children tire easily and cool down quickly. Frequent pit stops on the slopes for hot chocolate is always a good idea.

75. If you will be predominantly inside with smaller children who are too young to ski or get left behind in the afternoon while the older members of the family head off to ski, try to have some activities which allow them to remain as included as possible. This could include baking treats for when the family returns or creating a photo album scrapbook for the family holiday.

Chapter 7. Personal Conduct

As a travel nanny this could very often be the first time you have ever met the family and obviously both parties will have some nerves and apprehension. It is so important to conduct yourself to the highest possible standards.

76. Smile and having a positive attitude to every situation - your job is to enhance their holiday and keep their children safe and happy. Smiles and a positive attitude will put families at ease and let them know from the outset they've made the right choice in bringing you.

77. Manners!! It sounds obvious, but this is so important. Make sure you are making eye contact, greeting people, saying please and thank you, and offering to help where appropriate. This creates a very positive impression demonstrates to employers the positive influence you will have on their children.

78. Keep yourself, your possessions and sleeping area clean, tidy and presentable.

79. Diligence. Taking the time to ask questions to find out details of how parents would like tasks done and are there particular activities they want their child to partake in.   Similarly, if you have sole charge try to send regular updates and keep parents informed. Always ask permission before taking children anywhere that wasn't initially agreed or is outside of your accommodation.

80. Respecting boundaries and recognising family time. It is unlikely that a family will want you to be present 24/7 during a holiday and recognising a time when they might want some family time and you can fade into the background will be appreciated. If you aren't sure - ask!

81. Patience is key – situations and environments are always changing when travel and holidays are involvement. Patience and an ability to adapt quickly will stand you in good stead – prepare for the unexpected.

82. Being trustworthy. Employers expect a travel nanny to follow their rules of the household, even if the travel nanny themselves would not do things that way. They want someone who will keep the children safe and devote their attention to the children.

83. Dress appropriately for your surroundings.

84. Conduct yourself professionally during time off. It goes without saying that excessive drinking and drug-taking are unacceptable. To be honest it is a rare occasion when I would even drink one glass of wine during my time of employment. When offered alcohol by employers, I thank them appreciatively for their offer but reply that I do not like to drink when on the job.

85. Stay out of family arguments. At times holidays can be stressful and arguments can erupt between parents. Removing children from this situation where appropriate and remaining calm and understanding is important. Do not be drawn into arguments – a phrase along the lines of 'I'd rather not be involved if you don't mind' is a professional and neutral way of asking politely not to be drawn into an argument.

86. Following on from the above – be discrete – at no time as a travel nanny should you be gossiping about your employing family or passing on details of conversations that you have been privy to.

87. Restrain yourself with regards to your phone. Constantly checking your phone when with children or employers is unprofessional and could distract your attention from their safety. Keep your phone on loud and out of the way and focus all the attention on your children.

88. Resist the urge to check in on social media and post 'holiday' snaps. Families will want their privacy and these posts could potentially undermine your professionalism.

89. Ask permission before taking any photos of the children. As a rule, parents are usually delighted when you send them photos of their children happy and enjoying themselves but make sure you check first.

90. With the right age of children, a great idea is to make a holiday memory scrapbook with children – and parents absolutely love this too. Menu cards, supermarket receipts, ice-lolly wrappers, postcards, tickets to shows, even the odd photo etc. will make a great holiday activity and memory.

91. Very occasionally, employers make requests that make you uncomfortable or they could behave in an inappropriate manner. Depending on the nature of the situation it is important that you communicate neutrally, calmly and professionally and just explain your position and response. If the situation is serious contact your agency for advice or seek advice online.

Chapter 8. Post-Holiday

92. Make a fuss over the children and praise them effusively at the end of a trip. Personally, I believe positive encouragement with any age works wonders. At the end of the trip it's a great idea to give children a small keepsake or gift and write them a note or a card thanking them for the fun and telling them why they have been so great to look after.

93. It sounds obvious but maintain the work ethic and professionalism to the very last moment with your family - don't slack off near the end!

94. Express your gratitude at the end. Remember to say thank you to the family - they have put their trust in you (quite possibly a stranger to them a week ago!) and included you as a part of their family.

95. Make a record of the details of your trip. Include details such as payment, hours worked, duties, age of the children, destination etc. This is useful as a reference point and when demonstrating experience to future potential employers.

96. Following on from the above, make a record of what worked well in terms of entertaining the children, favourite meals, additional organisational tips etc. It is a good idea to list anything that perhaps didn't work so well and just reflect on what might improve

97. If employed through an agency provide feedback to the agency - letting them know if they were a great family to work for, the duties you carried out etc.

98. If paid by the family directly rather than the agency check that you have been paid the agreed amount. If not, you need to contact the family politely and firmly and explain the situation.

99. Quite often after a great family holiday with a travel nanny, parents will request to add you on social media sites. Consider social media requests carefully. Do you really want the family to have access to your personal life?

100. Ask your employers for some feedback e.g. any particular strengths they thought you had, can you use them as a reference on your CV if needed. Another option is to ask for a letter of reference which you can add to a folder of experience. Having a file full of great reference letters to bring and show to potential employers is a massive bonus.

101. Update your CV with this added experience before pursuing the next role - every little helps!

The End

Dear reader,

Thank you for taking the time to purchase and read this book – I hope you found it informative and enjoyable to read. I thoroughly enjoyed collating and writing about the advice I have collated over the past ten years.

If you have any comments, suggestions or corrections, feel free to send me an email to aefrey2013@gmail.com and I will consider your feedback before the next edition.

.

Made in the USA
Middletown, DE
11 March 2018